# NORTH WALES RAIL SCENE
## 1970s–1990s

### GARRY STROUD

AMBERLEY

*Front cover, top:* With its load of gunpowder vans from the explosives factory at Penrhyndeudraeth, 25-245 passes a lonely and deserted Morfa Mawddach station in charge of the returning weekly pick-up freight from Pwllheli to Shrewsbury on Tuesday evening, 19 September 1978. Previously numbered D7595, this loco was finally withdrawn in 1985 before being disposed of at Doncaster Works during 1986; *bottom*: On test from Crewe Works and making its first outing along the North Wales coast after receiving its new EWS livery, 37-426 runs round its stock at Bangor station before returning to Crewe on Wednesday 9 April 1997. Previously carrying the name *Y Lein Fach/Vale of Rheidol*, during the late 1980s and early 1990s, this loco was finally disposed of at C. F. Booth's scrap yard at Rotherham during 2013.

*Back cover*: At a favoured location for many railway photographers, EWS liveried 37-401 *Mary Queen of Scots* heads along the North Wales coast between Penmaenmawr and Penmaenbach tunnel in charge of the 08.36 Holyhead to Birmingham New Street service on the morning of Tuesday 22 September 1998.

First published 2024

Amberley Publishing
The Hill, Stroud
Gloucestershire, GL5 4EP

www.amberley-books.com

Copyright © Garry Stroud, 2024

The right of Garry Stroud to be identified as the Author of this work has been asserted in accordance with the Copyrights, Designs and Patents Act 1988.

ISBN 978 1 3981 1626 9 (print)
ISBN 978 1 3981 1627 6 (ebook)

All rights reserved. No part of this book may be reprinted or reproduced or utilised in any form or by any electronic, mechanical or other means, now known or hereafter invented, including photocopying and recording, or in any information storage or retrieval system, without the permission in writing from the Publishers.

British Library Cataloguing in Publication Data.
A catalogue record for this book is available from the British Library.

Typesetting by SJmagic DESIGN SERVICES, India.
Printed in the UK.

Appointed GPSR EU Representative: Easy Access System Europe Oü, 16879218
Address: Mustamäe tee 50, 10621, Tallinn, Estonia
Contact Details: gpsr.requests@easproject.com, +358 40 500 3575

# Introduction

To readers familiar with my first rail scene book, *Swindon Rail Scene, Hydraulics to HSTs*, this second title features images of an area that I have known since the mid-1960s, when family holidays introduced me to the North Wales rail scene. Being a West Country lad more familiar with the sound of Westerns, Warships and Hymeks, the unmistakeable sound of Class 40s powering along the North Wales coast was quite a revelation back then. Although during the 1960s it was more a case of noting the number than taking photographs, in the mid to late 1970s I began recording the North Wales railway scene on film.

Besides family holidays, work commitments also brought me to the area on many occasions during the 1970s and early 1980s, enabling me to document the railway scene in more detail. It was also at this time, during the winter of 1987, that I made a permanent move to the area.

Now with thousands of images taken over five decades, the photographs reproduced here represent a nostalgic dip into the past, when Class 40s, 25s, 37s, 47s together with first-generation DMUs were to be seen on both freight and passenger workings in the area. While the scenic qualities of rail photography in North Wales, particularly along the coastal sections and the Blaenau branch, are unsurpassed. Many of the images show not just the changing locomotive scene but also major infrastructure developments, with some locations completely altered by new building.

The photographs are arranged on a geographical basis starting from the west at Holyhead, and finishing in the Wrexham area to the east, also including the northern section of the Cambrian line, together with the Llandudno and Blaenau Ffestiniog branches.

All photographs are by the author.

*Garry Stroud*

With the carriage sidings on the left and the town of Holyhead in the background, the immaculate 47-638 *County of Kent* awaits departure with the 17.00 service to York on Sunday 22 February 1987.

Passing a freshly painted Holyhead signal box, 40-092 departs the town at 13.13 with a service to Manchester Victoria on Tuesday 26 June 1979. After withdrawal in 1982, 40-092 finally ended its days at Swindon Works, when during 1986 the loco was finally cut up.

The Class 01s stationed at Holyhead breakwater shed are recorded here on Tuesday 26 June 1979. Although slightly blurred due to my camera capabilities at the time and the low light conditions within the shed, this historic image captures 01-002 together with classmate 01-001 standing behind with its engine compartment covered by a tarpaulin. Out of use for a number of years, these two veterans from 1956 were both disposed of at Holyhead during 1982.

Climbing the 1 in 93 gradient out of Holyhead station, 08-907 is captured shunting empty stock on the morning of Wednesday 27 June 1979. Today 08-907 is preserved and resides on the Great Central Railway at Loughborough.

With the original cattle sidings still in situ on the left, and having passed the former steam shed, 45-118 departs Holyhead with the 17.03 service to York on Thursday 25 September 1986. Formally coded 6J in BR days, the shed and fuel bay stand rather empty awaiting the next occupant.

With an assortment of departmental vehicles on shed in the background, an eight-car DMU service comprising vehicles M51175, M56355, M50400, M56155, M56360, M51190, M56345 and M51176 enters Holyhead on the afternoon of Sunday 19 September 1976.

Surrounded by oil drums, 40-099 awaits its next turn of duty as it stands alongside the fuel bay at Holyhead depot on Wednesday 27 June 1979. With another five years of service left until withdrawal in 1984, 40-099 was eventually cut up at Doncaster Works the following year in 1985.

Another image captured alongside the fuel bay at Holyhead depot, where 25-265 carrying the unofficial bi-lingual painted name of *Castell Harlech-Harlech Castle* soaks up the winter afternoon sunshine on Sunday 15 February 1987.

After bringing in the 11.05 service from Manchester Victoria, 40-088 prepares to go on to Holyhead shed for servicing. With at least three Class 47s, a Class 08 and DMU in the distance, this busy scene was captured on Friday 29 June 1979. Withdrawn in 1982, 40-088 was finally disposed of at Crewe Works during 1988.

Almost twenty years on from the previous image, the cattle sidings on the left have long gone, together with demolition of the old steam shed, and in its place a new maintenance facility has been constructed. Photographed on Tuesday 16 June 1998, 37-414 *Cathays C & W Works 1846–1993* departs Holyhead with the 13.54 to Birmingham New Street.

The gates to the former cattle dock sidings have seen better days as 47-457 *Ben Line* enters Holyhead at 14.06 with the 09.50 service from Euston on Monday 10 July 1989.

The former Anglesey Aluminium factory on the outskirts of Holyhead dominates this scene on Tuesday 25 September 1990 as InterCity livery 47-483 passes with the 13.18 Holyhead to Euston service. To the right, awaiting departure from the works sidings, 47-229 *Springbok* has charge of eight cargo wagons bound for Warrington Arply yard.

Having just passed Valley station in the distance, 40-014 *Antonia*, minus its cast nameplates, heads an unidentified Manchester Victoria to Holyhead service on Thursday 24 August 1978. With just another three years of service left, being withdrawn in 1981, 40-014 was finally scrapped at Swindon Works during 1983.

Another view at Valley depicts 40-184 as it heads east with the 15.17 Holyhead to Manchester Victoria service on Tuesday 8 June 1982. Withdrawn the following December, this was the last year in service for this locomotive before finally being disposed of at Doncaster Works during 1983.

The open and flat landscape surrounding Valley and Rhosneigr is exemplified here, as 47-443 approaches Rhosneigr station with the 12.48 Holyhead to Euston service on Tuesday 8 June 1982. Lasting until withdrawal in 1993, 47-443 was finally disposed of at Crewe during 1996.

Passing Rhosneigr station, 25-304 heads east with an empty stock working from Holyhead on Wednesday 27 June 1979. Another Class 25 casualty of Swindon Works, this loco was eventually disposed of there during 1985.

Almost twenty years on from the previous image, not much has changed at Rhosneigr station as 31-113 approaches and heads east with the returning Valley to Sellafield nuclear flasks on Tuesday 16 June 1998. With its rather exposed position, Rhosneigr station is not the best place to be on a cold winter's day with a fierce north-westerly gale blowing off the Irish Sea.

Rhosneigr station can be seen in the distance as 150-133 in regional railways livery, together with 150-134 in all-over blue, accelerates away with the 13.23 Holyhead to Manchester Piccadilly service on Friday 12 March 1999.

Having staggered platforms either side of the level crossing, 47-480 is seen passing Ty Croes station with the 11.00 Euston to Holyhead service on Tuesday 29 August 1978. Just to the left of the loco, the white building was the former station master's house.

Having passed Bodorgan station, seen in the distance, 37-407 *Loch Long* has charge of the 14.30 Holyhead to Crewe service as it approaches Bodorgan tunnel and heads eastwards on Thursday 14 April 1994.

With the western portal of Bodorgan tunnel in the distance, 40-023 *Lancastria* approaches Bodorgan station with the 11.05 Manchester Victoria to Holyhead service on Tuesday 3 June 1980. Withdrawn just under a year later in May 1981, 40-023 was finally scrapped at Crewe Works during 1984.

The eastern end of Bodorgan tunnel is seen in this view as 37-422 *Robert F. Fairlie Locomotive Engineer 1831–1885*, making a colourful contrast with the yellow gorse, approaches with the 14.30 Holyhead to Crewe service on the beautiful spring afternoon of Monday 25 April 1994.

With the snowcapped mountains of Snowdonia in the background, 37-407 *Loch Long*, having just passed over Malltraeth viaduct, approaches Bodorgan tunnel and makes its way to Holyhead with the 13.50 service from Llandudno Junction on Monday 25 April 1994.

Possibly one of the most photogenic locations on Anglesey, the graceful arched viaduct at Malltraeth is the setting for this view as EWS-livery 37-421 has charge of the 10.07 Birmingham New Street to Holyhead service on Thursday 11 June 1998.

A roadside view of Malltraeth viaduct with Regional Railways Class 101 DMUs, 51506 and 53256, photographed on Wednesday 17 March 1999 en route to Holyhead with the 12.27 service from Llandudno Junction.

Approaching the village of Llangaffo, between Gaerwen and Malltraeth, 37-426 has charge of the 10.07 Birmingham New Street to Holyhead service on Thursday 18 March 1999. Withdrawn in 2003, 37-426 was finally disposed of at C. F. Booth's scrapyard at Rotherham during 2013.

*North Wales Rail Scene: 1970s–1990s* 17

Sprinter 150-250, together with Pacer unit 142-062, nears the junction for the Amlwch branch, and approaches the level crossing at Gaerwen, with the 10.00 Manchester to Holyhead service on Thursday 20 August 1987.

Not long after departing Amlwch, 47-323 makes its way across Anglesey with the returning chemical tanks from the Associated Octel plant en route to Llandudno Junction yard, and eventually to Ellesmere Port, at 12.35 on Friday 30 June 1989.

Looking in almost ex-works condition, although having lost her nameplate, 40-015 *Aquitania* nears Llanfair P.G. with the 12.48 Holyhead to Euston service on Friday 25 August 1978. With withdrawal coming in 1984, 40-015 was sent south to Swindon Works where, like many of its class, it had been reduced to scrap metal by 1986.

On the morning of Wednesday 4 June 1980 47-446 speeds through Llanfair P.G. station with the 10.09 Holyhead to Euston express. In the distance the old goods shed still stands together with a rather vintage carriage outside while a modern flat-roofed building has been constructed next to the original station.

Fast forward nineteen years and things have changed dramatically. Gone are the goods shed, coach and flat-roofed building and now a James Pringle store and car and coach park occupy the site. A Class 47 is still the motive power as 47-476 *Night Mail* with DVT 82147 *The Red Arrows* pass the station with the 09.19 Holyhead to Euston service on Monday 13 September 1999.

Llanfair P.G. station is in the far distance as 40-094 makes its way west to Holyhead with the 17.27 service from Crewe on the evening of Monday 7 June 1982. Just four months later 40-094 was withdrawn before being finally cut up at Doncaster Works during 1985.

With the Marquis of Anglesey's column dominating the view over the village, HST 43164, together with 43029 at the rear, is heading past Llanfair P.G. station in charge of the 09.50 Euston to Holyhead service on Thursday 30 October 1997.

Taken from the footbridge at Llanfair P.G. station, large logo 47-445 speeds past with the 09.20 Euston to Holyhead service on Tuesday 7 July 1987. Previously numbered D1561, the loco was withdrawn in 1991 and met its end at C. F. Booth's Rotherham scrapyard during 1994.

A bird's eye view of Bangor, photographed from above Belmont tunnel on Thursday 24 August 1978. An unidentified Class 47 departs the station with the 13.00 Euston to Holyhead service, while the Class 101 DMU is waiting to form the following all stations to Holyhead.

Looking in the other direction from the previous image, and photographed from above Bangor tunnel, 47-432 waits at Bangor station forming the 13.42 departure to Manchester Victoria on Monday 8 June 1981.

Emerging from Bangor's Belmont tunnel, 40-099 enters the station with an empty stock working from Holyhead on Wednesday 27 June 1979. Previously numbered D299, this loco was withdrawn during 1984 and eventually scrapped at Doncaster Works in 1985.

25-309 bursts out of Bangor tunnel with a train of empty freightliner wagons bound for Holyhead on Wednesday 9 June 1982. Renumbered during 1985 as 25-909, this loco is now fortunately preserved and resides at Peak Rail in Derbyshire.

On Friday 12 June 1981 40-132 soaks up the early morning sun at Bangor station waiting to propel its train out onto the main line before heading the morning parcel service to Manchester Victoria. Withdrawn in March the following year, 40-132 was taken to Derby Works and was eventually cut up by Vic Berry of Leicester.

Entering Bangor station, large logo 47-479 is in charge of the 13.05 Holyhead to Euston service on Monday 16 May 1988. With withdrawal coming just four years later in 1992, 47-479 was eventually disposed of at C. F. Booth's scrapyard at Rotherham during 1993.

Not exactly environmentally friendly with a cloud of diesel fumes engulfing Bangor station, six-car DMU, M50944, M56501, M50535, M56176, M56266 and M50983, makes a smoky exit forming the 11.57 service to Manchester Victoria on Monday 7 June 1982.

Making a rather unusual appearance for a Class 08 stabled in Bangor yard, Crewe-allocated 08-695 was photographed with the tunnel inspection train on Monday 25 April 1994.

Departing Bangor station, 40-034 formerly named *Accra* is in charge of the 11.12 service to Manchester Victoria on Wednesday 10 June 1981. Another three years' service was left for this loco before being withdrawn in 1984 and disposed of the same year at Doncaster Works.

Presenting a general view of Bangor station looking towards Bangor tunnel, Pacer 142-089, having just arrived at 15.55, waits to proceed with the 15.20 Holyhead to Hull service on Wednesday 19 August 1987.

Moving on to the Cambrian now, as four-car DMU, M50939, M56269, M56333 and M51203, passes the goods yard on the outskirts of Pwllheli in charge of the 10.42 service from Shrewsbury on Tuesday 19 September 1978.

The Cambrian has had a long association with the Class 37s and, although classed as 97s, they are still to be seen on the line today. Pwllheli station is the setting for this image as 37-427 *Bont Y Bermo* awaits departure with the 09.31 service to Euston on Saturday 16 June 1990.

On Tuesday 19 September 1978 25-245 is recorded in Pwllheli yard shunting its train of gunpowder vans from the explosives factory at Penrhyndeudraeth, forming the return pick-up freight later in the day back to Shrewsbury.

In the distance three passengers await the arrival of the 09.02 Shrewsbury to Pwllheli service, formed of DMU cars M50228 and M56055, as it enters Penrhyndeudraeth station on Wednesday 30 August 1978 at 12.24.

An image taken from the top of Harlech Castle records an unidentified four-car DMU having just arrived at the station with a Shrewsbury to Pwllheli service on Monday 5 August 1974.

The new order on the Cambrian as sprinter 150-140 departs Barmouth station at 15.04 with the 13.52 Pwllheli to Machynlleth service on Monday 25 May 1987. Note how the sand has encroached upon the sleepers and ballast at this exposed location.

The classic view of Barmouth Bridge, looking over the estuary of the River Mawddach. Photographed on the evening of Tuesday 19 September 1978, an unidentified two-car DMU is seen entering Barmouth with the 14.35 Shrewsbury to Pwllheli service.

Having departed the village of Fairbourne seen in the distance, a four-car DMU set, M56360 and M51176 in blue together with M56348 and M51188 in revised livery, makes for an interesting image approaching with the 10.34 Pwllheli to Shrewsbury service on Wednesday 20 September 1978.

With Aberdovey still retaining its classic BR name board, a two-car DMU, formed of M50398 and M56164, departs the station with the 14.35 Dovey Junction to Pwllheli service on Monday 18 September 1978.

Machynlleth shed yard is the setting here as 25-035 rests between duties and awaits its next working on Monday 18 September 1978. A DMU can also be seen in the shed in the background. Withdrawn in 1987, 25-035 is now preserved on the Great Central Railway at Loughborough.

Ten years on from the previous photograph, Machynlleth shed has lost its overall roof as Tyseley based DMU set T211, formed of M51937 and M54081, awaits its next duty on Sunday 1 May 1988.

After bringing in the Royal Train to Machynlleth as part of Queen Elizabeth II's visit to mid-Wales on Friday 11 July 1986, the two Class 37s, 37-430 *Cwmbran* and 37-426 *Y Lein Fach/Vale of Rheidol*, both in immaculate condition, run round at the station before taking the empty coaching stock back to Shrewsbury.

Back to Bangor now and along the North Wales coast, recorded on Wednesday 4 June 1980, 40-032 *Empress of Canada* waits to leave Bangor station at 19.25 with its service to Manchester Victoria. Withdrawn the following year, 40-032 became another casualty of Swindon Works scrapyard during 1983.

Emerging from Belmont tunnel, 40-162 passes on the centre road at Bangor with its train of cargo wagons from Anglesey Aluminium at Holyhead to Warrington Arply sidings on Monday 7 June 1982. With only six months' service left, 40-162 became another casualty of the Class 40 run down and was withdrawn from traffic in December the same year.

In ex-works condition from Crewe and having been named the day before, 37-407 *Blackpool Tower*, previously named *Loch Long*, made its first passenger outing in its new Transrail livery along the coast on Tuesday 21 February 1995. Hauling the 09.32 Crewe to Holyhead service, 37-407 is seen on its return working entering Bangor station with the 11.55 from Holyhead back to Crewe.

Passing alongside the Morfa Madryn nature reserve to the west of Llanfairfechan, large logo 37-408 *Loch Rannoch* approaches with the 17.18 Crewe to Holyhead service on the evening of Thursday 13 June 1996.

Painted in 1960s' green livery, 40-106 passes the western outskirts of Llanfairfechan with the 13.45 Manchester Victoria to Bangor service on Friday 12 June 1981. Today 40-106 is one of the lucky survivors of the class and can be found based at the East Lancs Railway.

Test trains from Crewe Works were for many years part of the North Wales coast scene and on Thursday 20 July 1995 47-767 was on test partnered with 47-781. They are seen here passing Llanfairfechan with their rake of Royal Mail stock working the return journey from Holyhead back to Crewe Works.

Another view taken at Llanfairfechan, although this time with the tide in, captures InterCity HST 43028, together with 43164 on the rear, in charge of the 08.58 Holyhead to Euston service on Tuesday 20 May 1997.

A long way from Network SouthEast territory, 47-583 *County of Hertfordshire* adds a splash of colour along the coast as it approaches Penmaenmawr station with the 12.55 Holyhead to Euston service on Saturday 14 May 1988.

Photographed on Friday 7 May 1999, DRS-livery 20-301 and 20-302 pass Penmaenmawr station with the afternoon Valley to Sellafield nuclear flask train. To the left at the end of the access lane the original goods shed then occupied by haulage firm Roland Young can be seen.

In an evening shot taken at Penmaenmawr on Friday 23 June 1995, having passed the station, 37-425 *Sir Robert McAlpine/Concrete Bob* passes the old goods shed as seen in the previous photograph with the 18.24 Crewe to Bangor service.

With practically all stone workings from Penmaenmawr quarry sidings heading east, this view taken on Thursday 20 August 1987 shows 45-046 *Royal Fusilier* having reversed out of the sidings and proceeding to head west with loaded ballast in connection with local engineering work on Anglesey.

Large logo 47-639 *Industry Year 1986* is photographed at Penmaenmawr quarry sidings on Thursday 5 May 1988. To the right preliminary work has already started on the construction of the A55 road upgrade.

Fast forward nine years from the previous image and the new A55 road has been completed and a busy scene is recorded at Penmaenmawr quarry sidings on Wednesday 23 April 1997. Three different locomotive liveries are pictured. 31-466 and 31-407 await departure with the 7F11 ballast to Warrington Arply yard, while 37-426 stands alongside.

On Friday 5 September 1997 an immaculate and freshly painted 56-114, now in EW & S livery, awaits departure from Penmaenmawr with the 7F11 ballast to Warrington Arply yard. Also of note is the recently applied English Welsh & Scottish name board at the platform end.

This photograph shows history being made at Penmaenmawr quarry sidings on Tuesday 25 May 1999. Marking the first appearance of a Class 66 to the site, 66-045 is seen during loading and eventually formed the return 6H10 ballast to Guide Bridge.

The old quarry workings stand out clearly in this image as InterCity 47-843 with DVT 82107 behind pass Penmaenmawr station and head east with the 09.19 Holyhead to Euston service on Wednesday 9 June 1999.

Departing Penmaenmawr with the 6F11 loaded ballast to Crewe, 37-419 with the unofficial name of 'Mt Pinatubo' pulls out of the quarry sidings and joins the Up main line as it heads east on Thursday 27 April 1995. For the record, Mt Pinatubo is a volcano in the Philippines.

Seen approaching Penmaenmawr on the evening of Monday 26 June 1995 31-142 has charge of the 18.24 Crewe to Bangor service. The footbridge known to local train fans as the 'iron bridge', which spans both the A55 and railway at this point, can be seen in the distance.

A very clean Transrail-branded 37-509, having just passed Penmaenmawr, approaches with the 10.23 Bangor to Crewe service on Saturday 24 June 1995. Previously numbered 37-093, this loco was finally withdrawn in 2001 and eventually disposed of at Cardiff Canton during 2005.

A lot has changed since this photograph was taken. The original A55 road on the left has now been replaced with the new dual carriageway where the sheep are grazing and the old gas depot in the distance has been removed. Photographed from the old iron bridge, 40-168 passes with the 11.57 Bangor to Manchester Victoria service on Friday 11 June 1982.

Fast forward seventeen years from the previous image and the changes are apparent and where once sheep grazed in the field to the left, now the new A55 makes its way along the coast. Photographed again from the 'iron bridge', 47-818 and DVT 82152 head east with the Virgin trains 09.19 Holyhead to Euston service on Monday 5 July 1999.

Travelling even further back in time and telegraph poles dominate the track side. This photograph, again taken from the old 'iron bridge', captures 25-186 heading east with an engineers' working from Bangor on Tuesday 3 July 1979. This loco became another Wiltshire casualty and was broken up at Swindon during 1987.

Sporting an experimental and unusual cab livery, InterCity HST 43028, together with 43029 on the rear, passes the same location as the previous image as they head the 09.00 Holyhead to Euston service on Friday 8 August 1997.

After emerging from Penmaenbach tunnel in the distance, 40-035 *Apapa* heads west with a Manchester to Holyhead freightliner working on the evening of Friday 11 June 1982. With only two years' service left, 40-035 was withdrawn during 1984 and finally disposed of at Crewe Works in 1985.

Making a brief visit along the coast on Tuesday 21 October 1997, departmental DMU 'laboratory 19', consisting of cars 977694 and 977693, has passed Penmaenmawr and is about to pass under the 'iron bridge' with a returning Holyhead to Crewe test run.

A last shot of this photogenic location looking towards Penmaenmawr captures a very clean-looking 47-810 *Porterbrook* together with DVT 82127 as they head east in charge of the 08.50 Holyhead to Euston service on Monday 1 June 1998.

Having emerged from the western portal of Penmaenbach tunnel in the distance, InterCity HST 43174 with 43166 on the rear head past the now demolished old roadside cottages alongside the A55, with the 10.20 Euston to Holyhead service on Thursday 18 May 1995.

The eastern portal of Penmaenbach tunnel forms this view as 37-037 heads towards Conwy with the 6F36 Penmaenmawr to Edge Hill ballast working on Monday 18 May 1998. Today this loco is safely preserved and based on the South Devon Railway.

With what appears to be some form of headboard on the front, 40-168 passes Conwy Morfa and approaches Penmaenbach tunnel with the 15.45 Manchester Victoria to Bangor service on Friday 11 June 1982. With just two years' service left, 40-168 was withdrawn during 1984 and finally disposed of at Crewe Works in 1986.

Nearly a decade has passed and things have changed considerably at this location – retaining walls in connection with the A55 dual carriageway have been built on the curve, not to mention Class 37s replacing the much-loved Class 40s. On Sunday 30 July 1995 37-425 *Sir Robert Mc Alpine/Concrete Bob* approaches with the 15.30 Crewe to Holyhead service.

With 47-761 on test accompanied by 47-972 *The Royal Army Ordnance Corps*, the pair head east past Conwy Morfa with the returning Holyhead to Crewe Works test train on Friday 21 April 1995. The old A55 road can be seen on the left with the new A55 road bridge crossing the railway in the distance.

Passing alongside the old A55 road at Conwy Morfa, 37-298 presents a colourful image against the line-side vegetation as it heads west with the 12.20 Crewe to Holyhead service on Saturday 12 June 1999. The bridge in the distance forms the link road off the A55 into Conwy.

In the 1990s fuel for use at Holyhead depot was delivered by rail. In charge of the returning Holyhead depot to Stanlow empty fuel tanks, 37-419, now having lost its unofficial 'Mt Pinatubo' name, passes Conwy Morfa on Saturday 13 May 1995.

With a view of Deganwy in the far distance, a bird's eye view from Conwy Mountain captures Loadhaul-livery 37-698, unusually in charge of the 14.17 Crewe to Bangor service, as it passes alongside the old A55 road at Conwy Morfa and heads west on Saturday 5 June 1999.

Bryn Morfa Holiday Park stands on the right, together with Conwy football ground on the left, as Transrail-branded 37-407 *Blackpool Tower* heads out of Conwy with the 18.24 Crewe to Bangor service on the evening of Monday 12 June 1995.

Heading past Cadnant cutting to the west of Conwy station, 40-137 finds itself in charge of the 11.05 Manchester Victoria to Holyhead service on Tuesday 3 July 1979. With just two years left in traffic this loco was withdrawn in 1981 and scrapped at Swindon the same year.

The same location pictured only eighteen years later and new houses have been built on the left and the telephone wires have long gone. In almost ex-works condition, 37-418 *East Lancs Railway* is seen at Cadnant cutting as it departs Conwy with the 15.18 Crewe to Holyhead service on Thursday 29 May 1997.

North Wales Rail Scene: 1970s–1990s    51

Conwy station is just visible through the arch as Dutch-livery 31-142 passes alongside Conwy's medieval town walls with the 13.23 Bangor to Crewe service on Wednesday 28 June 1995. Today this classic view is no longer possible due to excessive tree growth.

Photographed from Benarth Hill overlooking Conwy Castle, 37-429 *Eisteddfod Genedlaethol* emerges from the Conwy tube and proceeds west with the 12.41 Crewe to Holyhead service on Sunday 30 July 1995. Visible in the left corner and now demolished are the roof and buildings of Billington's Garage.

Passing Conwy town walls, 37-425 *Sir Robert Mc Alpine/Concrete Bob*, now in Railfreight Construction livery, approaches the Conwy tube with the 11.55 Holyhead to Crewe service on Tuesday 9 May 1995. The hand crane is all that remains of the goods sidings that once existed here.

Framed by the old hand crane at the end of the former dock sidings on Conwy Cob, HST 43164, together with 43028 on the rear, has just departed Llandudno Junction and approaches the Conwy tube with the 09.03 Euston to Holyhead service on Thursday 21 September 1995.

Conwy Castle forms the backdrop to this image, as 47-779 together with 47-635 cross over Conwy Cob and approach Llandudno Junction with the returning Holyhead to Crewe Works test train on Wednesday 19 June 1996.

Another image from the same location, as 60-017 *Shotton Works Centenary Year 1996* approaches Llandudno Junction with the returning 6H10 ballast working from Penmaenmawr to Guide Bridge on Monday 12 July 1999.

Adding a degree of interest to the London workings along the North Wales coast, Fragonset-livery 47-701 *Waverley*, together with DVT 82103, accelerates out of Llandudno Junction hauling the 08.30 Euston to Holyhead service on Saturday 29 August 1998.

Passing the old signal box (while the one in use today is being constructed alongside), 45-146 enters Llandudno Junction in charge of the 09.15 Bangor to Scarborough service on Friday 17 June 1983. Withdrawn during 1987, 45-146 was cut up in 1992 by MC Processors in Glasgow.

Having been held at signals, 47-351 finally gets the go-ahead and enters Llandudno Junction with an eastbound train of flat wagons, photographed on the morning of Sunday 19 September 1976.

With Llandudno Junction shed visible in the background, 40-199 departs the station with the 15.40 Manchester Victoria to Holyhead service on Monday 25 June 1979. With three more years of service left, 40-199 was withdrawn in 1982 and finally ended its days at Doncaster Works during 1983.

Taken from the top of the Station Hotel, this photograph shows a scene unrecognisable today following the development of the area. The sun has not long risen as 47-439 enters Llandudno Junction at 08.09 with the 07.09 Holyhead to Cardiff service on Friday 3 October 1986.

Outside Llandudno Junction shed, 40-141 awaits its next working as it takes a rest between duties on the morning of Tuesday 14 June 1983. The loco did not have long to go after this photograph was taken and was withdrawn four months later and eventually cut up at Doncaster Works during 1984.

Surrounded by freight wagons, 25-296 and 25-290 are photographed alongside Llandudno Junction shed on Friday 12 June 1981. Both locos were scrapped during the 1980s, 25-290 at Derby in 1983 and 25-296 by Vic Berry in 1987.

Crewe diesel allocated Class 08s, 08-921 together with 08-472 sporting the unofficial name of 'Injun Ifor', stand stabled for the weekend at Llandudno Junction yard on Saturday 8 October 1988.

It looks like Llandudno Junction shed has received a fresh coat of paint as 31-322 and 47-375 soak up the evening sun on Monday 22 June 1987. Demolished in February 2000, today nothing remains of the shed building and where locomotives once stood a cinema has been built.

On Friday 11 June 1982, with Llandudno Junction station looking almost deserted in the background, 40-160 has just arrived in the yard with four cargo wagons from the Anglesey Aluminium Works before continuing on to Warrington later in the day. Withdrawn in 1984, 40-160 was cut up at Crewe Works during 1987.

During the early 1980s, in connection with the construction of the A55 road scheme, Class 56s began hauling fly ash to Llandudno Junction from Fiddlers Ferry power station. Photographed on Thursday 28 April 1983, 56-067 prepares to reverse out of the yard with its return train of empties.

Long before the A55 tunnel was constructed under the River Conwy, the river at this point came virtually up to the stone wall. An eight-car DMU led by M56214 enters Llandudno Junction with the 10.50 Llandudno to Chester service on Sunday 19 September 1976.

Having just passed Deganwy station, 45-146 passes alongside the seawall and heads towards Llandudno Junction with the 15.16 Llandudno to York service on Wednesday 11 March 1987. Withdrawn the following month, 45-146 was finally cut up by MC Processors Glasgow in 1992.

Approaching the level crossing which once served as the road access to Deganwy Quay, 47-739 *Resourceful* heads back to Llandudno Junction with the empty stock off the Hertfordshire Railtours 'Llandudno & Bodnant' charter tour on Saturday 2 May 1998. Today a housing development occupies this site.

Passing Deganwy station, since demolished, 47-599 has charge of the 13.11 Llandudno to Euston service, on Sunday 2 August 1987. Today a car park occupies the site of the original station buildings, with bus-style platform shelters affording some protection from the westerly gales.

On Saturday 20 May 1995 the North Wales Coast Motive Power Day was held, featuring specials from Crewe to Llandudno and Bangor. The third special of the day was 20-075 *Sir William Cooke* and 20-128 *Guglielmo Marconi*, seen here passing Deganwy en route to Llandudno with the 13.05 from Crewe.

As an unidentified Class 150 is held at signals, Class 101 DMU set number CH 642, consisting of former Strathclyde-livery 53158 and blue-and-grey 51426, departs Llandudno with the 17.14 Llandudno to Chester service on Tuesday 21 August 1990.

At a time when Llandudno station had a complete overall roof, 40-117 awaits departure with the 16.42 service to Manchester Oxford Road on Tuesday 3 July 1979. Llandudno station car park now occupies this site. Loco 40-117 was eventually cut up at Swindon during 1983.

In this photograph from the North Wales Coast Motive Power Day on Saturday 20 May 1995, Class 37s 37-066 and 37-142, having arrived at Llandudno with the 15.05 from Crewe, reverse the empty stock into the sidings. Llandudno station even now retains its semaphore heritage.

In the early 1990s Class 20s made frequent visits to Llandudno with weekday services from Derby. On Monday 15 July 1991 it was the turn of 20-169 and 20-210, seen here departing Llandudno station and heading back to Derby with the 16.44 return service.

Accompanied by personnel from the Shell Oil Co., a naming ceremony was held at Llandudno station on Saturday 15 October 1988. Petroleum sector Class 47 47-324 was named *Glossidae* and 47-196 was named *Haliotidae*. They are pictured just after the naming ceremony with three oil-tank wagons and are still receiving admiring glances.

Back to Llandudno Junction, and having arrived with a test service from Crewe, an immaculate 47-816 *Bristol Bath Rd*, accompanied by 47-781 *Isle of Iona*, reverses out of Llandudno Junction yard before returning to Crewe on Monday 12 July 1999.

The atmospheric steam-age surroundings contrast sharply with more modern traction seen inside Llandudno Junction shed on Sunday 22 July 1990. Transferred here from Derby, stored Class 151 unit 151-004, together with 150-112, creates an interesting image.

The annual weed-killing service was always something different to photograph along the coast. Having visited the Conwy Valley and Blaenau Ffestiniog, 31-420, accompanied by 31-110 at the rear, enters Llandudno Junction on the way to Llandudno on Friday 16 July 1999.

Called the 'Roman Nose', Hertfordshire Railtours ran a special from Euston to Trawsfynydd on Saturday 18 April 1998, with 37-377, 37-098 and National Power 59-205 *L. Keith McNair*. Seen on its return journey, with the two Class 37s at the front out of sight, 59-205 is at the rear of the special as it heads back to Llandudno Junction and passes Glan Conwy.

Class 101 DMU M53308, M59125 and M53331 enter Tal-y-cafn station at 16.40 with the 16.10 Llandudno to Blaenau Ffestiniog service on Thursday 20 August 1987.

Adorned with a sign on the front stating 'Trawsfynydd Power Station the last flask 8 August 1995', 31-255 and 31-199 pass alongside the River Conwy and are seen approaching Tal-y-cafn station with the return nuclear flask working back to Llandudno Junction yard on this the last day of working, Tuesday 8 August 1995.

This is the same service seen in the previous image only this time on its outward run. Having obtained the single-line token at Llanrwst signal box (seen in the distance) for the section ahead to Blaenau Ffestiniog, 31-199 and 31-255 accelerate past Llanrwst North station at 07.25 en route to Trawsfynydd on Tuesday 8 August 1995.

A week earlier, on Tuesday 1 August 1995, it was the turn of 31-410 *Granada Telethon* and 31-130 doing the honours as they crossed the River Conwy between Betws-y-Coed and Llanrwst with the return flask working from Trawsfynydd back to Llandudno Junction yard.

Two-car DMU M56232 and M50949 wait to depart Betws-y-Coed station with the 12.25 Blaenau Ffestiniog to Llandudno Junction service on Saturday 18 September 1976. The waste ground on the right is now the site of the Conwy Valley Railway Museum.

After many years on the Cambrian the explosives traffic from Penrhyndeudraeth was transferred to the Conwy Valley line. Eleven years on from the previous photograph, the Conwy Valley Railway Museum is busy with summer visitors as 47-334 passes Betws-y-Coed station with the Llandudno Junction to Maentwrog Road freight on Thursday 13 August 1987.

Having travelled to Trawsfynydd from Llandudno Junction with the annual weed-killing service, 37-114 *City of Worcester*, together with 37-023 on the rear, is pictured approaching Dolwyddelan on the return journey back to Llandudno Junction on Wednesday 19 August 1998.

The scenic beauty of the Conwy Valley can be appreciated in this view, another photograph of the last return nuclear flask working on the branch. Having just passed Roman Bridge station, seen in the distance, 31-255 and 31-199 make their way back to Llandudno Junction on Tuesday 8 August 1995.

The slate tips and inclines are highlighted by the sun as Tyseley based three-car DMU M53055, M59611 and M53116 enter Blaenau Ffestiniog, passing the former LNWR station with the late-running 14.40 service from Llandudno on Wednesday 20 August 1986.

It was unusual to see a Class 37 and Class 31 combination on the flasks on Friday 5 May 1995. Following the failure of 31-304 at Llandudno Junction, 37-107 was found and together with 31-201 they are seen entering Blaenau Ffestiniog with the delayed outward-bound run to Trawsfynydd.

Having visited Trawsfynydd, 20-905 *Iona* is the leading loco with 20-903 *Alison* at the rear as they approach the former halt at Teigl with the return weed-killing service back to Llandudno Junction on Thursday 3 August 1995.

To the south of Blaenau Ffestiniog on the freight line to Trawsfynydd is Manod Viaduct, seen here on Thursday 3 August 1995. Hunslet-Barclay Class 20s 20-903 *Alison* together with 20-905 *Iona* on the rear cross the viaduct in charge of the annual Llandudno Junction to Trawsfynydd weed-killing service.

Back to Llandudno Junction now, on Friday 11 June 1982, 40-184 is in charge of the 12.07 Holyhead to Crewe service as it heads eastwards out of the station. With only six months of service left, 40-184 was withdrawn the following December and disposed of at Doncaster Works during 1983.

With the former railway allotments in the background, after bringing in a test service from Crewe, 37-415 together with test loco 47-785 *Fiona Castle* run round in Llandudno Junction yard on Monday 14 July 1997.

On the afternoon of Wednesday 19 July 1995 an unfortunate incident took place at Llandudno Junction. As 47-781 was reversing out of the yard with empty stock off a Birmingham to Rhyl charter, coach 5891 derailed, with the remaining coaches taken back to Birmingham by 47-583. The coach was rerailed the same evening by the Crewe breakdown unit.

Class 40 40-177, having got the signal to depart, pulls away from Llandudno Junction station in charge of the 17.40 Llandudno to Chester service on Monday 25 June 1979. Withdrawn during 1984, 40-177 became another casualty of the Crewe Works cutting crew in 1986.

Platform 1 at Llandudno Junction station is the setting for this image, as 31-512 prepares to depart at 09.32 with the 09.13 Bangor to Crewe service on Friday 23 June 1995. The siding to the right is still in use today and the occasional track machine is stabled here.

Approaching the outskirts of Llandudno Junction, 40-172 heads west with a Willesden to Holyhead freightliner service on Tuesday 14 June 1983. Another Class 40 destined for the scrapyard, 40-172 was withdrawn just three months later in September before meeting its fate at Doncaster Works in 1984.

In a photograph taken at Mochdre between Colwyn Bay and Llandudno Junction, 47-113 is seen heading west with another Willesden to Holyhead freightliner service on Wednesday 15 June 1983. The construction works on the left are in connection with repositioning the new railway line at this location and the existing track which the Class 47 is on eventually becoming the new A55 dual carriageway.

Fast forward to 1995 and the change at this location is dramatic. The original rail route is now the A55 dual carriageway, as 31-439 *North Yorkshire Moors Railway*, together with 31-465, heads past Mochdre with the 11.24 Crewe to Holyhead service on Tuesday 8 August 1995.

With one lane closed in each direction on the A55, it seems that traffic is being kept to a minimum as 47-840, accompanied by 47-489 'Crewe Diesel Depot Quality Approved', approaches Colwyn Bay with the return Holyhead to Crewe test train on Thursday 6 April 1995.

Closed in 1991 and demolished in early 2000, Colwyn Bay signal box is seen here as 47-539 *Rochdale Pioneers* approaches Colwyn Bay station with an eastbound freight from Llandudno Junction yard on Tuesday 22 March 1988.

On Friday 3 February 1995, 37-425 *Sir Robert Mc Alpine/Concrete Bob* catches the winter sun as it departs Colwyn Bay station at 12.51 with the 11.55 Holyhead to Crewe service.

Having emerged from Penmaenrhos tunnel in the distance, InterCity livery 47-843 and DVT 82147 *The Red Arrows* pass Llysfaen, east of Colwyn Bay, with the Virgin Trains 09.19 Holyhead to Euston service on Tuesday 14 September 1999.

Llandulas Viaduct is the setting for this scene, as, fresh from Crewe Works and on test, 56-110 *Croft*, unbranded but in Loadhaul orange-and-black livery, accompanied by 47-766 *Resolute*, heads towards Abergele with the return Holyhead to Crewe Works test train on Monday 31 July 1995.

With Abergele in the distance, Mainline-livery 37-274 adds a splash of colour to the North Wales freight scene heading west with the 7D06 Guide Bridge to Penmaenmawr empty ballast working on Tuesday 17 June 1997.

Another freight service worth going out to record was the Humber Oil Refinery to Holyhead petroleum coke working. Seen here approaching Abergele, Immingham-based Class 37s 37-058 and 37-694, formerly named *The Lass o' Ballochmyle*, head east with the return working from Holyhead on Thursday 29 June 1995.

It wasn't always sunshine, sea and sand on the North Wales coast as this photograph portrays. Following a light dusting of snow, 37-407 *Blackpool Tower* passes the station at Abergele with the 09.32 Crewe to Holyhead service on Friday 3 March 1995.

Framed between the two Down line semaphore signals to the west end of Abergele station, 37-415 approaches with the 10.48 Holyhead to Birmingham New Street service on Friday 10 September 1999. Hired in to supplement services during the summer, the chocolate and cream coach makes for an interesting contrast.

Passing on the Up fast line through Abergele and Pensarn station, the original name board visible on the wall to the right, 25-125 heads east with the 13.00 Llandudno to Manchester Oxford Road service on Saturday 30 June 1979. Four years later, 25-125 was to end her days at Swindon Works and was scrapped there in 1983.

With the Up fast line now lifted, a brief glimmer of sunlight illuminates Abergele station before the approaching rain as Fragonset-livery 47-709 with DVT 82101 make their way to London Euston with the 08.50 Virgin service from Holyhead on Friday 23 October 1998.

Showing off its new Railfreight red-stripe livery, 37-680 approaches Abergele station with the outward Crewe Works to Llandudno Junction test working on Thursday 16 April 1987.

Passing Abergele signal box, Transrail-branded 60-015 *Bow Fell* heads west with the 6P26 Guide Bridge to Penmaenmawr ballast empties on Tuesday 14 September 1999. Today the Down loop has been removed with an extension of the station platform forward to the line the Class 60 is on.

Painted in 1960s green livery during the mid-1990s, Celebrity Class 101 set 101-685, Nos 53164, 59539 and 53160, approach Abergele station with the 07.12 Crewe to Llandudno service on Thursday 10 August 1995.

In Regional Railways Merseyrail livery, 150-211 adds a splash of colour along the North Wales coast and having departed Rhyl station in the far distance, approaches the marine lake heading west with the 09.55 Manchester Piccadilly to Holyhead service on Friday 23 October 1998.

Although the lines into the bay platform at the west end of Rhyl station have been taken up, the rusty remains of the goods yard sidings still remain, as 47-435 departs the station with the 09.48 Crewe to Holyhead service on Thursday 16 April 1987.

On test and fresh out of Crewe Works, 56-024 is put to front-line use and makes its passenger debut along the North Wales coast. Accompanied by 47-640 *University of Strathclyde*, it enters Rhyl station with the 09.20 Euston to Holyhead service on Friday 30 January 1987.

Passing Rhyl No. 1 signal box and photographed just half an hour later than the previous image, 45-140 approaches Rhyl station with the 08.20 Newcastle to Llandudno service on Friday 30 January 1987.

The Down semaphore signals have already been removed, although the Up line is still in use, as North Western Trains-livery 158-753 departs Prestatyn station in charge of the 12.16 Manchester Piccadilly to Llandudno service on Wednesday 14 April 1999.

Having just passed Prestatyn station in the distance, 31-233 *Severn Valley Railway* together with blue-livery 31-450 head east with the 6F36 Penmaenmawr to Edge Hill loaded ballast working on Wednesday 12 June 1996.

Making a perfect match of clean Regional Railways locomotive and stock, 37-429 *Eisteddfod Genedlaethol* has just passed under the main A548 coast road bridge at Prestatyn, and approaches with the 12.18 Crewe to Holyhead service on Saturday 15 June 1996.

On the skyline in the distance are the buildings of the former Point of Ayr colliery at Talacre as 37-402 *Bont-y-Bermo*, together with chocolate and cream coach 5030 behind, passes alongside the seawall at Ffynnongroyw with the 12.22 Bangor to Crewe service on Saturday 8 June 1996.

Comprising one cargo wagon from Holyhead and two Tunnel Cement wagons from Bangor, 47-537 *Sir Gwynedd-County of Gwynedd* passes Mostyn Docks with the daily trip freight bound for Warrington Arpley yard on Thursday 16 July 1987.

Mostyn Docks forms the backdrop to this image as 37-420 *The Scottish Hosteller* passes alongside a rather empty A548 coast road in charge of the 13.22 Bangor to Crewe service on Saturday 8 June 1996.

On many occasions there were surprises on the Crewe Works test trains and Wednesday 17 July 1996 was no exception. Having just passed Mostyn, 47-846 *Thor*, in light-grey undercoat and accompanied by 47-530, heads back to Crewe with the return test run from Llandudno Junction.

A regular Class 20 diagram during the 1980s was the MGR traffic from Fiddlers Ferry power station to Point of Ayr colliery. Approaching Mostyn, 20-010 and 20-175 have charge of the westbound empties working on Friday 9 September 1988.

A landmark along the coast for many years, the *Duke of Lancaster* ship is seen in the background. Showing the old and new Regional Railways livery variations, 156-420 and 158-757, in the revised colours, are seen approaching Mostyn on Saturday 8 June 1996 with the 13.17 Manchester Piccadilly to Llandudno service.

Held at signals, the driver heads back to the cab of 47-376 as he awaits clearance to proceed at Holywell Junction with the daily trip freight from Llandudno Junction yard to Warrington Arply sidings on Friday 9 September 1988.

Returning to Crewe Works from Llandudno Junction after a test run along the coast, Royal-livery Class 47s 47-798 *Prince William* and 47-799 *Prince Henry* make for an interesting comparison with the Royal Mail stock as they pass Holywell Junction on Tuesday 17 September 1996.

Following engineering works in the area, 40-174 and 40-055 are recorded at Mold Junction on Sunday 6 June 1982. Both locos did not have long to go, with 40-055 withdrawn just five months later, while 40-174 lasted until May 1984. Both were eventually cut up at Doncaster Works.

Approaching Buckley, 56-129 is in charge of the 6F41 Warrington yard to Dee Marsh logs on Friday 23 August 1996. This loco was scrapped at Hartlepool during 2011.

Passing Penyffordd station on the Wrexham to Bidston line, a very clean Loadhaul-livery 37-710 heads the returning Dee Marsh to Mossend empty timber wagons on Monday 22 September 1997.

Again, on the Wrexham to Bidston line 56-089 passes Cefn-y-bedd station with the 6V78 Dee Marsh to Margam return empty steel working on Thursday 27 August 1998. Withdrawn in 2002, this loco was cut up by C. F. Booth at Rotherham in 2009.

On the site of the closed Croes Newydd depot at Wrexham, 47-201 and 25-253 await their next turn of duty when photographed on Sunday 6 June 1982. Today, both locomotives have also been consigned to history, with 47-201 scrapped in 2007 and 25-253 in 1985.

With its rake of blue-livery British Steel wagons making a striking impression on the North Wales freight scene, 56-044 *Cardiff Canton Quality Approved* approaches Wrexham General station with the returning 6V78 Dee Marsh to Margam steel empties on Friday 6 September 1996.

Recorded heading south past Wrexham General station this time on Wednesday 4 September 1996, Transrail-livery 56-115 is captured with an older rake of wagons hauling the 6V78 Dee Marsh to Margam returning steel empties.

Railfreight coal-livery 60-061 *Alexander Graham Bell* climbs up Gresford Bank heading south towards Wrexham, where reversal will take place before heading north on the Bidston line with the Elgin to Dee Marsh logs on Thursday 21 April 1994.

Passing Wrexham General station, 47-237 comes off the Bidston-line light engine and heads south towards Shrewsbury, on Wednesday 28 April 1993. Today this loco is owned by West Coast Railways.

# Also available from Amberley Publishing

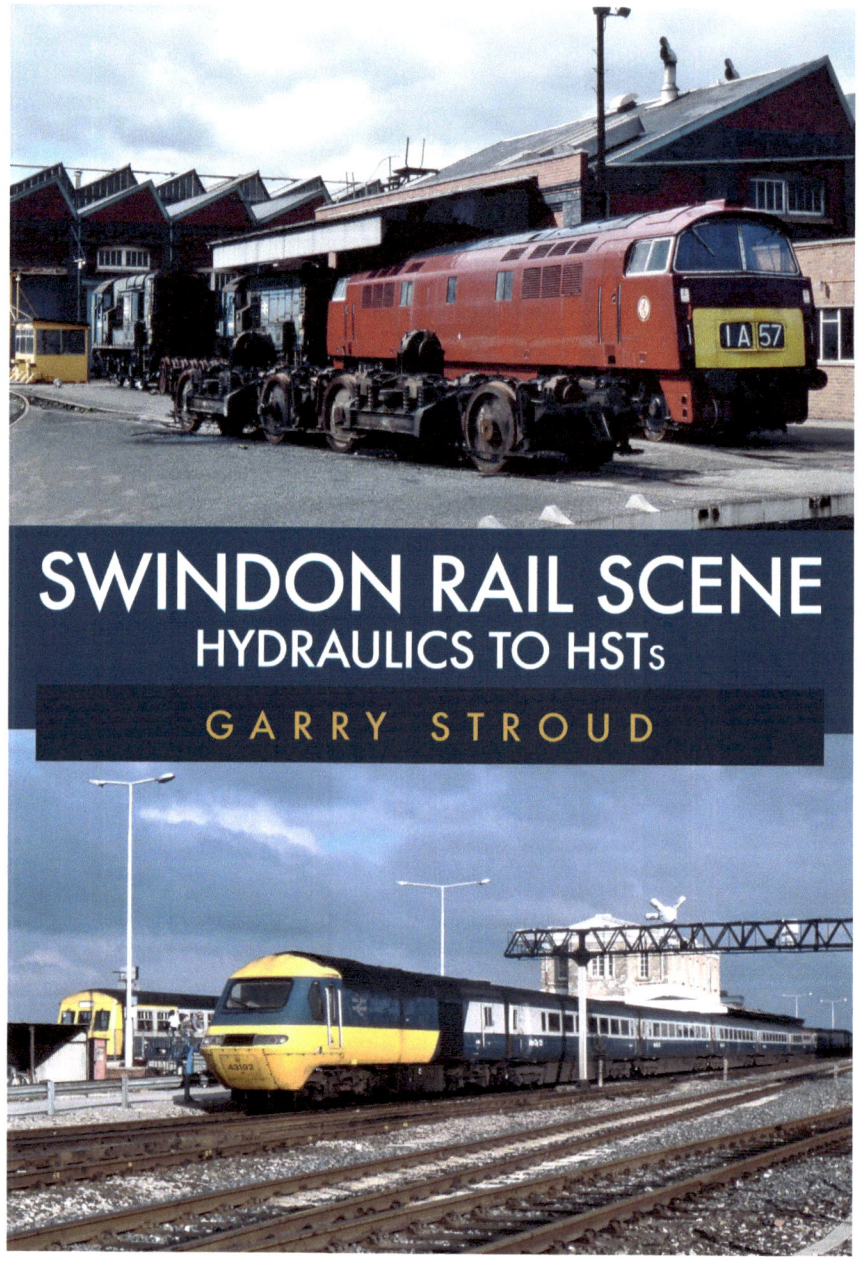

Fantastic colour photographs, taken by an ex-employee of Swindon Works, looking at the Swindon rail scene.
978 1 3981 0054 1
Available to order direct 01453 847 800
www.amberley-books.com